MW00578896

The full beauty of the rose is already present in the bud—

Swami Radha at age 19.

the rose ceremony

swami sivananda radha

timeless small books
2004

timeless
www.timeless.org

in the US:
P.O. Box 3543, Spokane, WA 99220-3543
info@timeless.org
(800) 251-9273

in Canada:
P.O. Box 9, Kootenay Bay, BC V0B 1X0
contact@timeless.org
(800) 661-8711

Edited by Swami Gopalananda
Book Design by Colin Dorsey
Thanks to Andrea Rollefson for photos

Printed in Canada on acid-free paper
Previous Printings: March, August 1997
2nd Edition

Library of Congress Cataloging-in-Publication Data

Radha, Swami Sivananda, 1911– 1995
  The rose ceremony / Sivananda Radha.— 2nd ed.
    p. cm.
  ISBN 1-932018-03-4 (alk. paper)
  1. Hinduism—Rituals. 2. Roses—Religious aspects—Hinduism. I. Title.
  BL1226.72.R33 2004
  294.5'38—dc22
                                2004001584

table of contents

part 2 continued

conclusion

God, here is a flower. I have not made the flower. I have no power to create a flower. I have really nothing, not a single thing I can call my own. But I take this little part of your creation and I give it back to you, charged with my love, my emotions and my devotion. Please accept my offering.

—Swami Sivananda Radha

introduction

the hidden power of the rose

The seed for the Rose Ceremony was planted many years ago during Swami Radha's time in India. She often saw rose petals being used in the worship of Divine Mother and in Pada Puja (worship at the feet of the guru). Although she was personally reluctant to emphasize the ceremonial or ritualistic aspects of worship, she saw that a simple ritual could be a means for expressing the very fine feelings that can emerge from gratitude and humility. One day in Dehra Dun, where she had been sent by her guru, Swami Sivananda, to learn Indian dance, she spontaneously created a rose-offering to him out of a deep feeling of gratitude for all that he had given to her. Back in the West, when she was asked by some of her Catholic devotees if there was a ceremony they could incorporate into yoga that would honour the Virgin Mother, it was quite natural for her to respond from her experiences in India. From this early impetus, her ideas for the Rose Ceremony began to take form.

With the Rose Ceremony, Swami Radha has created an original way for us to make a personal commitment or dedication to an ideal. Revelation of the beauty and power of the ceremony rests entirely in how each of us experiences the process. Elaborate or simple, the purpose of the ceremony remains the same—to create a means for remembering. Your sincerity will open the door to your experience of the Rose Ceremony.

The following pages describe the different symbolic aspects of the Rose Ceremony as they would appear in an actual ceremony. Swami Radha's commentary in each section is composed from several Rose Ceremony talks she gave over the years. Her words can serve as a starting place for your own journey into the hidden meaning of this most beautiful ritual.

—Swami Gopalananda

how to do a rose ceremony

You can have a Rose Ceremony privately for yourself,
or you can bring a few people together to have one as a
group. There is no particular time of year; you may have a
Rose Ceremony whenever you feel the need to make or
renew a commitment. A Rose Ceremony creates its own
special space, but you can help it do so by choosing a place
that is already special, perhaps the space where you do your
own spiritual practice. As you make your preparations, you
may wish to think of each step as an offering to Divine
Mother.

You will need two vases of red roses on your altar. One contains enough roses for everyone taking part, and the other an equal number as an offering to Divine Mother. You may wish to sit near the altar and hand a rose to each participant, or you may allow participants to take their own rose from the vase. Also, have two lighted candles on the altar. Nearby, have a crystal bowl of water.

To help create a receptive atmosphere for the ceremony, chant a mantra or have a quiet period of meditation before it begins. To begin the ceremony, everyone chants the healing mantra, *Hari Om*. The chanting continues until all have completed the dedication of a rose.

When you feel ready, you go to the altar to receive your rose. Take it to the bowl of water, and then begin to remove the petals one by one. Place each one into the water. As you do this, repeat softly to yourself the pair of opposites each petal represents, and ask for Divine love in return. Pairs of opposites may include, for example, love and hate, health and sickness, generosity and selfishness, anger and compassion. It helps to make a list beforehand of the pairs that seem relevant to you at this time.

When all the petals have been removed, the center remains, the part of your rose to which the opposites were attached. At this point you may cut the stem with the scissors, leaving the center of the rose attached, and place the two pieces beside the bowl. Or you may cut the center off the stem and place it in the bowl with the petals. Both actions reflect a degree of commitment. You are free to choose whichever seems appropriate to you at this time.

When everyone has dedicated a rose, the chanting of the *Hari Om* mantra will come gradually to an end. The petals may be left in the water overnight, if you are doing the two parts of the ceremony over two days. Take them out of the water in time to let them dry before the second half.

It is helpful to have quiet time to yourself between the first and second parts of the ceremony. During this time, make a list of your grudges and resentments and have the list ready for burning.

The second part of the ceremony needs *prasad* (a special sweet made or bought for the celebration), a small ladle for giving each person a sip of the water, and a fireplace or somewhere suitable to build a fire. Make the fire ahead of time so it will be hot, and place the tray of leaves, stems and rose petals close by. Each participant will also need two small containers, one watertight. The mantra *Om Namah Sivaya*, to Shiva, remover of obstacles, can be chanted throughout this part.

When you're ready, take your list of grudges and resentments to the fire and place it in the flames, together with a handful of petals, leaves and stem, to be consumed once and for all in the fire of wisdom. On returning from the fire, go to the altar to receive a sip of the water in which the rose petals were placed.

When everyone has been to the fire, the chanting comes to an end, and *prasad* is given out. Repeating together the mantra of the Divine Light Invocation brings the ceremony to a close. Later, after the fire has cooled, you can collect some of the ash and some of the rose water. The ash will remind you that once old resentments are burned to ash they ought to remain so and not be resurrected anew. The water will be available any time you feel a need for it. You'll be surprised at how fresh it tastes, even months after the ceremony.

—Swami Gopalananda

part one

entering the symbol

where it began

$\mathcal{T}$he first flowers I bought for my Guru, Swami Sivananda, in the bazaar in Rishikesh were roses. When I returned to the Ashram, I saw that the thorns on the roses could injure him, so I removed them all before giving the flowers to him. When I handed the roses to him, he put his hand out to accept them, and then suddenly he pulled his hand back.

"The thorns!" He said.

"There aren't any," I replied. "I have removed the thorns so that you wouldn't be hurt."

"Ah!" He said. "You understand."

But I must be frank; I did not understand. My actions were simply done out of consideration for him; if I brought something to him or did something for him, I felt that it should not make pain, period. That was my attitude at the time. A few days later he said to me, "Divine Mother will take away many thorns from your life."

Just before leaving India, I was in Kailas Ashram, which is the starting point for the pilgrimage to Mt. Kailas, home of the ice-cave abode of Lord Shiva. The leader of Kailas Ashram knew I was leaving in a few days, and he looked at me very seriously, nodding his head, and then he turned to a man standing nearby and said to him, "Get all the rose petals from the morning worship of Divine Mother and give them to her."

The young disciple went to the temple, gathered up a whole bunch of rose petals, knotted them into a good piece of cloth, and gave them to me. And then the head of the Ashram said to me (he always had his mala in his hand), "Every day I will give you one round of the mala to support your work. There will be many blessings for you in the work for the West." Then he looked at me very seriously and continued, "It will be very difficult, very difficult. At this moment you cannot even envision how hard it will be. But don't worry, you are protected." As I look back, I can see that he was a person of great wisdom.

Later, when I was back in Canada, I asked myself, How can I put some of these experiences together into a ceremony with the rose? I remembered a prayer Ramakrishna made to Divine Mother. On each bead of his mala, he would say, "I give you my health and my sickness, give me Divine love in return; or I give you my wealth and my poverty, give me Divine love." He would say this prayer for all the pairs of opposites that came to his mind. I thought if I remove the petals from the rose, each one representing a pair of opposites, and place them into a bowl of water asking for Divine love in return, that would be one way. And the center of the flower is like the hub of the wheel; all the petals are attached to the hub. If I take the center and put it into the water with the rose petals, then perhaps that could be a way to make the suggestion to myself that I can become one with my own inner Light. Having experienced the rose as one, but also the perfume of the rose as one, I wanted to have that oneness that doesn't change—a rose remains a rose. I had to ask, How can I get to that place in myself, knowing that the established religions cannot help?

I think you can see from my own experience with the rose that there can be considerable power in a symbol. And, of course, building a ceremony around the symbol led me to look much more deeply into my own experience, which was a real confirmation for me of the path of freedom I had chosen.

ceremony—the means to remember

India has a lot of very lovely rituals dedicated to Divine Mother, and it was after seeing some of them that I was able to bring ideas for the Rose Ceremony back to the West. According to our Christian background, Mary, whom we also call the Queen of Heaven, is our form of Divine Mother. In the East, Divine Mother is called Shakti, the creator of all that is manifest. In India it is recognized that all power manifest comes from the one source. In other words, the power and its manifestation are inseparable. By way of illustration, we could say the flower and the scent in the flower are inseparable. And so each one of you, male and female, is inseparable from the Divine power. To help establish that idea in your mind, the Rose Ceremony is both a dedication and an acceptance of that power at the same time.

However, you cannot have a personal relationship with a power that is impersonal to you. Once that power manifests, you can love the power in its manifestation. But you can only have cosmic consciousness if you have accepted Divine Mother's creations in all her forms, not just the beautiful and the satisfying.

The decision to do the Rose Ceremony is, of course, a very special one. In order to make it, you must clearly see the questions before you: Do you want to be rooted in the pursuit of something that gives you some satisfaction and a place in the world, or do you want to be rooted in Divine love? Nothing grows without being rooted in something. By doing the ceremony for yourself, you make a decision about where you want to be rooted in this life, and that is very important. Such a decision will follow you throughout your life.

–swami radha–

In the Rose Ceremony, the questions are concerned with ideals and the purpose of life: Why was I born? What is the purpose of my life? Why am I here? What kind of person do I want to be? What makes my life worthwhile? To begin to answer such questions, you have to make your priorities clear, and that means starting to make decisions. Sometimes priorities may overlap or be so close that a decision may be rather difficult to make. It is important to understand, however, that making a decision strengthens us. Even if we make a wrong decision in life, we can learn from our mistakes. Courage and willingness to take a stand come from that learning.

The ceremony is a means to dedicate yourself to the Most High. It is not a promise to anyone or anything else but that. However, it is not one of those ceremonies or initiations that are for the rest of your life. The Rose Ceremony can be repeated. Next year, when roses bloom again, you can repeat it. If you feel a need for it, you can repeat it sooner. This is all up to you. It is your decision. But even a temporary dedication can make a great deal of difference in your life. You know where you are going.

the rose as symbol

*Y*our own unfolding is like that of the rose. First, there is a seed that has to germinate and put out roots. All of this takes place beneath the soil, long before you can actually see anything happening. The roots grow deeper into the ground to get a firm hold and to get nourishment. Where are your roots in this life? What are you rooted in? These are important questions to think about.

Next, a little green shoot, very tender, breaks through the soil and into the light. After the shoot has grown a little more, the first two leaves appear. They are coarse, but the leaves that come after are more and more refined, until finally the first bud appears. As the bud slowly expands, the flower begins to emerge, until one day it is fully open. I think of this symbol of the rose as a lovely metaphor for your own growth, and eventual spiritual unfolding.

Symbolism is linked with thought association, and in this particular ceremony we have a very rich and meaningful symbolism. The Rose Ceremony is a means of guiding your thinking, your interpretation, and eventually your understanding into greater depth. Interpreting symbols according to your personal experience can reveal the depth of knowledge and experience that is already in you. Symbols, like scripture or inspired poetry, expand your capacity for understanding—sometimes I call it the light of understanding. Your interpretation and experience of a symbol is the starting place to that deeper understanding. The symbolism of the Rose Ceremony is an opening for you into your own thinking.

part two

the ritual

water and the crystal bowl

Placing the rose petals and the center of the rose into the crystal bowl of water is an act of surrender. Water can be associated with cleanliness and purification, the water of life. You surrender to the water of life, and this is all beautifully symbolized by your intent and your actions in the Rose Ceremony. The water becomes holy through this concentration of intent and also by chanting the mantra. Overnight, the pairs of opposites become purified, and in the morning this water will be distributed.

After the Rose Ceremony, you are still a human being who has to struggle along the path, using discrimination and doing the best you can at any given moment. To remove yourself from the pair of opposites—punishment and reward—is a tremendous undertaking. But as you begin, you will find that God's grace supports you, and if you put forward even a little effort, you will become aware of how readily available that grace is to you.

The scissors you use to cut the stem can remind you of your power of discrimination, the power to cut off the ego. In everything you do in life, you should use as much discrimination as you can. Think things through and you won't make too many mistakes.

–swami radha–

candles

The two candles represent your two selves: the physical, material self that is tied up with all the personality aspects, and your Higher Self. Each candle is nourished by the same Light. But where there is light, there is also shadow. My physical body obstructs the light, creating a shadow, but my shadow does not have a life of its own separate from my body. The energy, which is neutral, creates both and comes from the same source.

The material-physical and the mental-spiritual all exist by the power that comes from the one source. So do not let this division that you sometimes feel stand in the way. My shadow and I are not really separate. The underlying energy of life is the same, even though that energy manifests in many different ways.

rose

The rose is a most beautiful flower, sometimes called the
queen of the flowers, and it commands all of your senses.
Eyesight participates by being enchanted with the beauty
of the rose, and you can feel the velvety softness of the rose
petal between your fingers. The perfume of the rose travels
through the air. Can you see it? No. Spiritual perfume travels,
too, and some people with a good sense of smell can perceive
the spiritual perfume from another person. The rose is
satisfying to your sight, emotions, touch, smell, and even
to your taste. Rose oil is used in marzipan or almond paste.
Rose oil is very precious. You need to press many pounds of
rose petals for just one drop of oil.

Our earliest associations with roses equate them with
love. For each of us, the word has a particular meaning, and
it is good to clarify for yourself what you mean by love. For

example, when do you call an emotion love? If I help a couple to stay together for the sake of their children, is that love? Or is it compassion for the children's future? When does love become so impersonal that you are willing to help under any circumstances? It's hard to say. Perhaps the best thing is not to think so much about love, but to develop instead a high degree of concern and consideration for others.

Why do we use red roses in the ceremony? Red is the color of blood, the very life force itself. You can live without food for quite awhile and you can live without a lot of comfort, but if you were drained of the last drop of blood your brain would collapse. There would be no more thought—however Divine—not even a prayer. Red stands for life, and life has to be accepted, not denied. By accepting the give and take of life in the proper sense, and by establishing your ideals, you enrich yourself and make your life worth living. When you have done this, you have little or no fear of death because you know you are doing your best. Life is then seen as most precious because each time we come into a life we are given another chance. It is God's love that gives us the opportunity again and again to keep on trying.

–swami radha–

petals

The center of the rose is the sun, and the petals are the infinite but harmonious diversities of Nature. Our nature is made up of personality aspects and the force of opposites, which are represented in the rose by the petals.

As you remove each petal, you think of it as representing a pair of opposites, and you offer that to the Divine, asking for love in return: "I offer my knowledge and ignorance, and I ask for Divine love in return. I offer the positive and the negative in myself, and I ask for love. I give all my feelings of love, all my feelings of hate, and all the degrees in between, and I ask for Divine love in return." We could have the world with all its wealth and power. But if we did not have love, we would be very, very poor. It is in giving—in the true giving of ourselves and in the true sharing of whatever we have—that we receive.

It is the play of opposites in us that creates never-ending conflict. This continual movement between the opposites means I am constantly going back and forth between punishment and reward. Now I give them to the Divine because in the past I have not handled the resulting conflict very well. When we remove the petals in the way that we do—as an offering to the Most High—then the work of transformation is given direction and a next step. Almost nowhere else can you find this next step presented so tangibly in the path of Higher Consciousness.

stem

The stem of the rose represents the spine and the flower is
the head. A spine that is light and straight (but not inflexible)
can be an indication that one's thinking is straightforward—
facing life straight on and not getting bogged down by
negative characteristics. This does not mean having a stiff
spine as opposed to being spineless. The stem of a rose is
not rigid. I compare it to the flexible trunk of a willow tree,
which can survive a storm because it can go with the pressure
of the wind while the hard, rigid oak can break in the same
storm. It is not a matter of having enough will to bend or
resist; it is where we choose to apply all the will that we do
have. This is where discrimination comes in.

Let your spine be straight. If you can walk straight with
your head erect, that means you have nothing to hide. The
posture of your body, or even of a child's body, indicates a

great deal. A child, already worried for whatever reasons, will slump in a chair, shoulders stooped, staring at the ground. It is no use to tell this child to sit up straight because the slumping is not the problem, only the symptom. Watch people walking: How do they move? Very few are really straight and direct.

When you have finished removing the petals of the rose, you can cut the stem in half with scissors, thinking at that moment that you are cutting off a large portion of the ego. The two pieces of stem can be placed on the tray with the leaves, and later offered back to the fire.

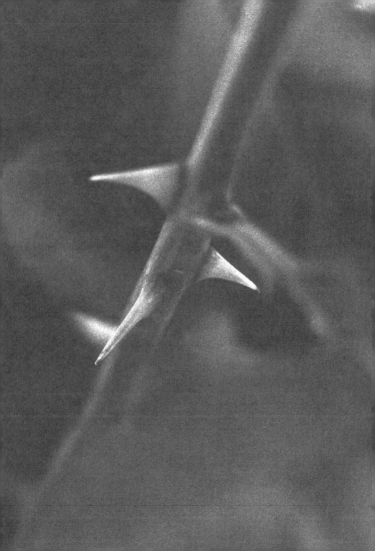

thorns

The rose, as beautiful as it is, has something else besides the beauty. Thorns. If you try to grab the rose, the beauty of life, you may be hurt. The thorn is also symbolic for the ego and the mind sticking out from beneath the beauty and the soul. However, you can use the thorn to remove the thorn. If you want to know yourself and be free, you can use mind to investigate mind. You can use your selfishness constructively and investigate yourself using the process of reflection. Reflect on the events of your day, and if you are not satisfied, make changes. This is very different from judging and condemning yourself. Being overly critical is just as bad as not being critical at all. Proper criticism can come in your reflection when you find the facts and you deal with them as best you can so that you can rest assured in yourself. Reflection is a wonderful means for making the conscience clear.

I have a beautiful old picture of a human being sitting on a lotus, holding a long-handled mirror. The picture is saying something about reflection. How does my face reflect in the mirror? Do I see a face of kindness, or greed and jealousy? Do I see a face that is trustworthy? Do my eyes reflect God's Light or do they anxiously seek recognition? Your daily reflection can ask: "How have I passed this day and how can I learn from the possible mistakes of this day?" Learning means seeing what is, which requires going beyond condemnation and judgment. We learn by trial and error; in fact, all great things in life have been achieved by trial and error. The only real sin in life may be the intentional repetition of mistakes once they have been seen. To help reinforce our sincerity, we can offer the thorns to the Divine as we remove them, asking that it be the Divine who removes all the thorns from our life.

Many times that I have done the Rose Ceremony at the Ashram I have removed the thorns before the roses were to be used. When some people commented about this, I said, "I'm not Divine Mother, but I hope even in this gesture that I can help remove some of the thorns from your life so that

–swami radha–

you won't be wounded by all of them." You can do the same for others. Whenever you give someone a gift of roses, take the thorns off beforehand with the thought that this is what you wish in your heart for the one to whom you are giving the gift.

leaves

Everything has its season. At the Ashram, July is the month when the roses bloom.

In time, everything comes into flower; even your love. The seed already contains the rose. Eventually, after the seed germinates, the first two leaves appear. The second pair of leaves is more refined than the first, and as the plant grows the ascending leaves become more and more refined until finally the flower appears. Slowly the flower unfolds, taking its own time, seeming to sense when the conditions are right. The plant has to work to produce the stem, the leaves and the flower. Cause and effect are all around us. From the seed to the first pair of coarse leaves, then finally to the flower—we can observe a process of evolution in miniature.

The process of evolution is around you and in you, and you cannot exclude yourself from it. Is it possible, then, for you to cooperate with this process of evolution? Yes. The power of choice is definitely yours. If you cooperate with the process of evolution as it pertains to you as an individual, your life will go considerably more smoothly. If you do not cooperate, knowing that you have a choice, then destiny can very easily take you by the neck and shake you to the bone, and there is ample evidence that this is what happens. On the other hand, many people can achieve something important in life only when they are put under great pressure. Without the pressure they do not exert the effort. The choice, however, is definitely yours. You don't have to be shaken.

–swami radha–

center——the essence

If you decide to put the center of the rose into the water, that can be seen as a dedication of all you are to the Most High, and I want to emphasize that that is what you surrender to. All the initiation ceremonies of the East are never meant to be a dedication of one human being to another; they are meant only to bring you into contact with the divinity within yourself and help you to take the last steps to Liberation. My initiations—mantra, brahmacharya, and sanyas—were not a promise to my guru. The obligation between my own guru and myself is only to support each other where possible.

It is a tough decision to dedicate yourself completely to the Divine because you know that it is serious and it carries a lot of weight. However, once you have dedicated yourself to the Most High, you have a destination in life and you are no longer floundering like a leaf bouncing on the waves of life here, there and everywhere and not belonging anywhere. You have a destination and a means to get there, and that is the beginning of your path of Liberation. All actions in the Rose Ceremony will have a lasting impression if you are sincere.

fire

Mind has an awesome power, and if that power is bound up in long-held grudges and simmering resentment, then the road to liberation is simply closed. Fire, which is symbolic for light, wisdom and passion, also destroys the ignorance that fosters grudges and resentment.

Why is it so important to free our selves from grudges and resentments? Mind has an awesome power, yet the power itself is neutral. Even the power in resentments when stripped of resentment is neutral; it depends on what you do with this power. The mind can be a master, a taskmaster and a slave at the same time. If the power of the mind is given to an ego that constantly seeks changes and schemes for self-gratification, such a mind is considered to be impure. A teacher in the East does not think of the one who has never made a mistake as having a pure mind. No. The person who has sufficient awareness to live by his or her own highest ideals and ethics and who maintains that awareness through daily reflection and introspection is approaching the state of pure mind. Through the power of mind, human beings are co-creators with God.

When we become aware of our own grudges and resentments, it is useful to remember that there are lots of people who may have plenty of reason to hold grudges and resentments against us. We, too, have created the circumstances. The Rose Ceremony presents an opportunity to free yourself from the chain of attachment that is forged through your resentment toward another. Yoga is the path of liberation, and it's a glorious path for anyone who understands what is required to be free.

If your choices in life are always determined by the ego, then you'll miss the entire purpose of this lifetime. Some pleasure is not only justified; some pleasure is acceptable and right. But a life of selfishness is a great tragedy. If the ego is allowed to grab all the power that comes from prayer, then the serpent of wisdom becomes the serpent of evil, caught in

–swami radha–

an endless round of temptation. Wisdom or temptation—the power of choice is there for every individual.

In the temples in India, all the rose petals are collected for burning in the temple fire. As long as you live between punishment and reward and the resulting myriad of opposites, you don't have Divine wisdom. Put some petals into the fire along with your paper listing your grudges and resentments, with the understanding that ignorance, living in the realm of the opposites, is burned in the fire of Divine wisdom.

And you must not take the grudges and resentments back. You are offering these things to the Most High in return for Divine love, and that offering is like a promise. You must keep your promises, whether they are made to another person or they are in the form of a dedication of your own life to the spiritual path. But the most serious promises to break are those you make to the Most High.

If you feel that you are sincere at the time, and the temptation of resentment comes back, then resort to prayers. Put yourself into the Light and ask for your own mind, your heart and your emotions to be illuminated sufficiently to let go. To the degree to which you can let go of your resentments and your grudges, you will be set free. That is what you have to remember. That is what the Rose Ceremony is all about.

–swami radha–

prasad

Divine wisdom is sweet because it takes away the bitterness of life. Through Divine wisdom you learn to see the other side of life, not just the pain. When the bitterness is removed, you can experience the inherent sweetness in life. The sweet that I am giving to you now is called prasad. Giving *prasad* also means that I am giving you a promise: to share everything with you that I know, to help you and further you on your spiritual path.

conclusion

growing into light

*M*ost of the time we are unaware that we are
walking in God's Light. Sometimes life looks very
dark. But after many long, dark, winter days, the first spring
day comes with its first spring flowers and we think a miracle
has happened. It was a very glorious day in my life when I
met my Guru, Swami Sivananda. After years of searching in
the dark, suddenly many things began to come to life. Swami
Sivananda and my experience in India held many answers for
me. Perhaps without the darkness I would never have
appreciated the Light.

My wish, and also my prayer for you, is that the Light will guide you and heal your body, your mind and your emotions, and that your awareness and understanding will grow into that new Light, and finally that you will become a Light unto all those whom you meet. In the end, true knowledge and awareness is what makes you spiritual.

Om Om. Om Tat Sat.

–swami radha–

–swami radha–

about the author

Swami Sivananda Radha (1911–1995) is the author of ten classic books on yoga, including *Kundalini Yoga for the West, Hatha Yoga: The Hidden Language,* and *Radha: Diary of a Woman's Search.* She is also the founder of *ascent* magazine. After being initiated by her teacher, Swami Sivananda of Rishikesh, Swami Radha returned to North America in 1956. She started the Yasodhara Ashram in Canada and dedicated her life to updating the Eastern teachings for the Western mind.

For more information call Timeless Books (800) 251-9273 (www.timeless.org) or Yasodhara Ashram (800) 661-8711 (www.yasodhara.org).